HOW

HAPPY

DO

YOU

WANT

TO

BE

?

COURTNEY BEEMAN

Built To Last Publishing LLC
Copyright © 2020 by Courtney Beeman

Printed in the United States of America.

SERIES OF EVENTS

Introduction:

Just felt like I needed to start this off letting you know I do not believe in regrets. I am a firm believer that everything, and I mean every little thing happens for a reason. With that being said, I wouldn't change a thing about my past. This is simply to let you know that we all go through things in life but what matters is how you grow through it.

God has blessed me in so many ways. We may not always know our strengths, but He does. With Him, all things are possible.

chapter 1: growing pains

-Give it your **best** shot-

3 Keywords of This Phase
1. patience
2. optimistic
3. family

What's the 1st thing that comes to your mind when you think of high school? Mine is, "Oh Lord!" That's not to say it was all bad. Of course, I have great memories of it, but it was the most trying time for me. I swore I knew everything and had to do things my way. Great advice came to me from pretty much everyone around me, but I didn't listen. For some reason I just had to learn the hard way.

I went into high school with high expectations. I just felt like it had to be the best time of my life. It was a completely different atmosphere from middle school. We had just moved to a whole new city the year before, so it was a little difficult making new friends. I came into a place where most people had been going to school for years together and being new wasn't always the easiest.

Regardless of how it started I still felt like I wanted to be included. I honestly made an effort to create memories and enjoy being a teenager, even though I was out of my comfort zone.

I remember a time I dated this guy in high school. And this was late-middle school/early high school so I use the term "dated" very loosely. Back when things were really just about talkin' on the phone all the time. Sneaking on the phone at night since my dad didn't want me talkin' to boys yet. Once I was "of-age" we talked a lot more and planned to see each other at get-together's, since he's a family friend.

I was on the phone talkin' to him one day and all of a sudden, his mom got on the phone asking who I was. I told her my name and she started asking me questions. He was close friends with my cousin, and he told her who I was. She said, "Oh do you go to the hall, Courtney?" I said "No, I don't." She replied, "Oh well 'he' don't talk to people who don't go to the hall" and hung up on me.

I couldn't believe it. Don't get me wrong I was well aware we had different beliefs. My family has been divided more than half my life based on religion, so I wasn't immune to it. But this had never happened to me before so abruptly. I cried my eyes out to my mama and she understood too well.

This woman basically told me I wasn't good enough to talk to her son because I was not a

Jehovah's Witness. It crushed me. Not necessarily the ending of the relationship, like I said we were kids, so it wasn't that deep. It was the fact that I felt dismissed because we didn't share the same beliefs.

Up until that point I'd never felt like I wasn't good enough for someone. I always felt like I was a great person with a lot to offer, but she made me feel so small. Like I didn't even matter.

I did my best not to dwell on it and ended up getting past it. I knew there was nothing I could do to change how it made me feel at that moment. I couldn't hold on to it. I had to make sure I didn't let her opinion affect me. I had no reason to take it personally. She didn't even know me.

When I look back on it now, I know it happened for a reason. All that taught me was that I'd never be the one to dismiss someone because of their religion. I'd never want to make anyone feel they're not worthy. Who am I to judge? There is nothing that makes me superior over someone because of who I worship. My beliefs are my own and everyone is entitled to their own, without judgement.

Believe it or not there are still so many people who feel this superiority. But I'm not here to change anyone's beliefs. It's sad to think this has been going on for so long but I'm sure it will continue to be the same. I know that we're all human. And whether we "go to the hall" or not that does not make us bad people. It doesn't matter who you give praise to, we are all the same.

There is no award for putting someone down. This is not something to be proud of. I don't know why people think it's okay to determine someone else's worth by what they believe in. These ways have caused a lot of friction in my family and it's honestly disheartening. But it's so common, it's just become the normal.

Sometime later in high school life, I was in a situation I had no business being in. It didn't matter how many times anyone told me to walk away. It wasn't until years later I learned the magnitude of what was going on. Luckily, I was able to come out of it with a new mentality- "When everybody is saying the same thing, listen. They not all wrong!"

At that age it was no way for me to have it all figured out. I was still going through things that required maturity I had yet to find. I had a hard time with the word NO and struggled to cope when things didn't go my way. In hindsight, there were many times I could've been in danger, but I felt invincible. My sister and I had a great life growing up, so to some extent I thought nothing could go wrong.

Friends and family definitely got me through those times. And through rough times you find out who your real friends are. Being teenagers, every little thing seems way bigger than it is. I couldn't always see what mattered. A lot of times I would get wrapped up in the moment and let emotions get the best of me. It was hard for me to pace myself and think things through.

All I really wanted to do was hang out with my friends. Yes, we did have a lot of laughs and adventures, but I really should have been more involved in other activities. Something outside of the high school drama and gossip would've been good for me, but I never really thought about it at that time.

I went through a vocational program to make sure I could spend less time at school. I loved doing hair so I thought cosmetology would be a great fit. The experience itself was one-of-a-kind. The hands-on environment really provided a boost of confidence I never knew I needed. The friends I met there made it fun. It was such a great time, from hour 1 to 1500!

I spent a lot of time trying to make things go my way. It just felt like I had to be in control of every situation I was involved in. So much emotion consumed me through those 4 years, and I just couldn't understand why back then.

Grudges were held against people that may have made decisions based solely on what was right for them at the time. That was hard for me to understand because my mind didn't operate like that. I felt like I was a pretty good friend to those around me. So, once I felt like the friendships weren't even, I had no choice but to remove myself.

Things could have been a lot easier through my teenage years if I wasn't so against anyone else trying to help me. And not help in a sense of doing something for me but help in the form of guidance. The wisdom that was passed on to me, should have really made a difference at that time. It just went in one ear and out the other.

If I knew then what I know now I would've told myself right along with everybody else, "Courtney, let that boy go." I would tell myself to focus on me and figuring out what I wanted to make out of my life. Had I spent a little more time worrying about myself than what friend I was mad at, I would've been in a better position to figure out my life after high school.

Now I can completely comprehend "agree to disagree". Everyone around does not have to agree with what you're saying or doing. Just as we're entitled to our own opinions, so are they. I also understand when my mama said "Everybody ain't yo friend." Going through the drama while it was happening, I couldn't grasp that. I felt so strongly about my friendships and relationships that when things fell apart, I fell apart. None of that was worth falling apart. I understand that now.

My decisions from all those years ago do not define me. They are just part of my story. The times spent and memories made will always play a part in making me the woman I am today.

For anyone currently going through high school, please take your time making decisions. There is no way you can have your whole life figured out at your age, and that is okay. Patience is key. Have faith that what you're doing right now will pay off in the long run. The steps you're taking to progress are so necessary and they **require** time. Everything in due time.

If you're ever in a situation where everyone is telling you to get out of it, please do so. I was fortunate enough to come out of dangerous situations unharmed, but everyone is not as lucky. Please listen to your parents and family. If they're anything like mine, they only want the best for you and believe me they are speaking from experience.

We are all going through life the best we can. Choose to make every moment count, and when you get to be my age, you'll appreciate it so much. High school is such a precious and delicate time. I didn't really understand that before. Although every decision at that time does not dictate your life, many of them do guide you towards where you want to end up.

Know that you are strong enough to overcome any obstacle in your way. Now **I'm** speaking to you from experience. Things will all work out how they are supposed to. If things are not working out how you planned with your friends or spouse, please make sure that these people have your best interest at heart. Spend your time doing what you love and figuring out what type of person you want to be when you grow up.

The power to be successful in your life is held by you. You are the designated driver on this road trip called "life" and don't let anyone take that away from you. This is your show, so you call the shots. But don't get so carried away calling the shots that you can't accept advice or appreciate guidance from someone who has done this before. Please don't worry. This is only the beginning of your journey!

Now tell me, after taking some time to reflect, what order would you prioritize the keywords from the last phase?

PATIENCE   **OPTIMISTIC**   **FAMILY**

1.______________
2.______________
3. ______________

Why?

chapter 2: on your own two feet

-Chin up baby, smile for the camera-

3 Keywords of This Phase
1. self-discipline
2. determination
3. connections

Central State University was the best thing that ever happened to me! Hands down- amazing experience from start to finish! I could talk about it for days, but I won't lol! It wasn't perfect, but I feel like the experience was made for me. I needed to see life through an HBCU!

I honestly had no plans to even go until the last minute. I hadn't figured out where I wanted to be in my life, but this felt right to me as soon as I got to campus. I had no idea what to expect since I had never lived away from home, but I was so excited.

There were so many people from all over. I felt like I was in one big melting pot. Getting to meet people from different places and backgrounds was one of my favorite parts. Before then all I knew was life in Michigan and had no idea about things outside of my sheltered home life.

I never realized how dependent I was on my family, before I went away. The little things like making a dentist appointment or making sure I got up in time for class were literally all on me. It was a shock at first to adapt to having all this new-found freedom, but once I figured out these were all my responsibilities now, I adjusted.

Me and my girls were always tryna eat good. At one point eatin' good to us was just anywhere off campus. We went in town one time to get some fast food and walked right into an eye-opening experience. There were multiple employees there, of a different race. I think it was

4 or 5 of us and we all took a second to look at the menu and see what we wanted.

Now we all practiced something called common courtesy, so it was only natural for us to speak to them. No one spoke back to us. When we came in they stared at us in silence like they never seen anyone like us before. I found that hard to believe since we were only ten minutes away from our campus. But there was no common courtesy returned. Just blank stares. No words to even acknowledge they were hearing our orders right.

We all knew what was going on and felt the discomfort. But when another group of people walked in, of their same race, they were completely different people. Before then we didn't even know they could smile. They were so friendly and courteous to them. So polite. We actually heard words out of them.

We waited for our food and just seen a whole different staff of people basically. When our food was up, they just sat it on the counter and walked away. Didn't even mention it. Only reason we knew it was ours was by looking at the receipts on the bags.

These people couldn't even fix they mouth to say hello to us. Racism was and **is** still alive. I had never experienced it first-hand. It put me on edge immediately. My first year in school, first time away from home, around people who couldn't stand us. Ain't even know nothing about us, but we didn't deserve to feel welcomed in that establishment.

I learned quickly to be aware of my surroundings especially if we were going in town. That was not the only place that gave us those blank stares, but it was the first. At school we were in our own little bubble away from the outside world. But right outside our yard there were people against us, all because of the color of our skin. And they had no problem making it known how they felt about us.

We were lucky to have had the confidence not to let them discourage us. And we were not going to stop going certain places because of them. We knew how to handle ourselves. We made sure their actions did not determine ours.

Even now to this day, **racism is still alive**. It's insane to think this would still be a topic of discussion all these years later. It's a shame to think there are still so many people who don't like you and even try to hurt you because of the color of your skin.

As long as you know you're a great individual, what anyone else thinks shouldn't matter. I know discrimination hurts, but those people are miserable. They don't have the intelligence to look past color. They lack the courage to practice right from wrong. All we can do is focus on being the best version of ourselves.

Don't let their narrow minds distract you from reaching your full potential!

After getting a routine down between class and enjoying campus life, I realized taking control of my future was something I could handle. I never doubted I would do well in school, but I didn't know what college life would entail. My roommate and suitemate were the best and really made me feel comfortable in our new home. There were a lot of firsts for all of us experiencing freshman year and I'm so grateful I got to meet them.

It wasn't until I got to Central that I was forced to learn self-motivation and self-discipline. These are two things I know for a fact helped me succeed. At 18 I had to figure out how to keep pushing through on days I may have felt overwhelmed. I had to make sure my priorities were in order.

Self-discipline was required to make sure I could manage my time wisely. I had to set aside time to get all my classwork done, study for tests and exams, all while networking to make the most out of this new experience. I found by motivating myself to get up every day, more determined than the day before, anything was possible.

Friends were essential being away from all my family. I had no idea I was creating friendships to last a lifetime. Everything was so new at first and I couldn't have picked any better friends to go through this journey with. At this stage I felt way more comfortable with creating bonds than I did in high school. Here we were young women and men ready to take on any thing that came our way, and no one was going to stop us.

The more devoted I became to learning who I was as a college student I noticed new things about myself every day. I didn't have many situations growing up where I had to be resilient and outgoing but when the time came for it in school, I surprised myself. I showed up for me. Every minute of every day. And I knew that as long as I kept my focus on my goals, I would get to wherever I wanted to be.

Things were not always great. Of course, there were still lessons to be learned while becoming a young adult. If anything, this was the most crucial time to be figuring things out. There were situations that took place where it was easier to revert back to responding out of emotions as opposed to handling things rationally. I was so used to getting what I want and still trying to find ways to accept things when I didn't.

I turned to the University counseling services for assistance with coping with the changes I was going through, and it was the best decision of my life. I met a counselor there and he helped me sort through so many feelings I was having. He gave me an outlet. Yes, I had friends and boyfriends too, but sometimes I just needed to talk to someone impartial. Someone that would not judge me for my past mistakes. And of course, I needed someone else to talk about problems I'd had with friends and boyfriends.

He also helped me figure out ways to overcome any issues I was having with family back home. We went over positive steps to help me continue to succeed in my classwork. We worked through issues from the past that may have affected how I was coping with similar issues in the present day. Regardless of what we discussed I never felt ashamed of asking for help.

Although most of the time I felt like I had it all figured out, I had to be open to the fact that it was okay to reach out to someone who can offer more guidance. Someone who could see things more clearly from the outside looking in. There was no issue with seeking assistance to better myself. Counseling was my saving grace, and I am forever grateful for the experience and the way it has changed me.

The ability to allow someone else to see who you are with no prior history requires complete acceptance. You have to be able to accept who you are in the space you are in. You have to be willing to admit that you don't have all the answers and love yourself enough to be open to someone else helping you figure things out. It's okay to accept help. You don't want to deny yourself any chances to grow and become a better person.

In order to give yourself the best shot at making things happen you have to be confident enough to listen to other's opinions. Just because someone is not telling you what you want to hear does not mean they're wrong. I had to learn my way of thinking was not always right. Once I grasped that my mind was open to so many different outlooks on life.

We have to be able to motivate ourselves on a daily basis. You want to make sure that you don't get in a habit of relying on other people or other things to motivate you. And that goes for everyone, not just college students. We need to be secure in ourselves. We as individuals have to instill determination in ourselves as we grow and prosper.

This stage of late teens into 20's is the time for us to really get to know ourselves. It is the prime time for you to try new things and figure out what works for you and what doesn't. Don't get stuck thinking you should be way more ahead in life than you are. We have to move at our own pace. It's only right that we each have our own road to success. It's up to you find out what your version of success looks like. Use this time to take advantage of the trial-and-error period.

It's okay if you don't know exactly what you want to do in your life. The key is to at least explore different opportunities so you can make an informed decision. There is no rule that says you have to know your life plan as soon as you graduate high school.

Take this time in your life to get comfortable relying on yourself. Make sure that you are okay with handling your daily responsibilities. It may be a lot to take in at this transitional stage, but it is all part of the process. We've all been here before so just know you're not alone.

Come up with ways to make sure you're keeping up with what you want to accomplish regularly. For me, I have to write everything down. Goals, tasks, notes you name it. I'm best organized when I have everything written out and can keep it all in front of me.

If this is where you are in life make sure you **soak it all in**. Stop and smell the roses baby, your 20's are like no-other. Use every day to get you closer to your goals. This time is valuable and cannot be wasted. We're all a work in progress but as long as you **keep** pushing you are destined to make your dreams come true. Put in the work and dedication and no one will be able to stop you from succeeding.

Once it's all said and done it will be worth it. Going through the process of coming into your own is rewarding in itself. If you're just starting this phase it may not seem like it at first but trust me this will be an unforgettable time. Live it up and please, make sure you **enjoy** it!

Now tell me, after taking some time to reflect, what order would you prioritize the keywords from the last phase?

SELF-DISCIPLINE   **DETERMINATION**
CONNECTIONS

1. ___________
2. ___________
3. ___________

Why?

chapter 3: real world

-Take control of **your** life, and accept **your** fate-

3 Keywords of This Phase
1. soul-searching
2. grind
3. responsibility

And what are we to do now? If you're anything like me, you may be thinking this or had this thought before. Some people plan out their life early on, or they may just figure it out in their own time. Don't be discouraged if you're still wondering what is next for you and where to go from here.

I've always loved writing and knew it was something I wanted to do. Once I got to college I was interested in Psychology and couldn't decide between it and English. I did my major in English

Literature and minor in Psychology and to this day I am still fascinated with both aspects. I wasn't sure if I wanted to go into teaching English or becoming a therapist. I took classes to help me explore both fields.

I loved college life so much I never wanted it to end. When it came time for graduation, I was still unsure of what road I wanted to travel. Eventually I went back home and got comfortable in my "safety net". I felt like I needed to get in the right head space to regroup. Just as much as it was an adjustment going to school, it was sort of a shell-shock after school. So, I went back to what was familiar.

In order to keep the goal-oriented mentality you have to keep thriving as much as you were before. I went home and went straight to working and sooner than later got caught up in paying bills. My daily routine had changed drastically. I wasn't seeing my friends on a regular basis since we lived in different states. I wasn't going to classes anymore, or eating at the caf, going to parties. It was a whole new world for me. It wasn't a bad thing, but it put a delay on me figuring out what the next steps in my life would be.

Before I knew it the daily grind of a 9-5 consumed me. I never really took the time to think about what I wanted to do now that I was in the "real world". I knew I needed to make a plan and get the next phase started but for some reason I just couldn't figure out how. All the tools that helped me thrive in school were not being put to use and it was no one's fault but my own.

I went through multiple jobs and could never really stay happy at most of them for too long. Not realizing I was constantly searching for signs to lead me to my destiny. Signs to help me figure out how to get out of this confusion. I still felt confident in the positions I held, but nothing ever really felt like it was meant for me.

I didn't understand how to be the same driven and motivated person once I got home. I wasn't writing out my list of goals or making sure I was focusing on my self-improvement. It was always work and family. Work and family are definitely on the list of top priorities, but because I wasn't thinking about how to advance in life it felt like I had nowhere to go. I always thought before I was climbing the ladder of success. Once I felt like I didn't know what I was working towards there was no drive to keep pushing. I had no clue on what to do next or where to turn.

All I really could do was be the best at the jobs I was working at. That brought some solace. For the time being it was okay when I could push to advance at work. I had no idea I was stuck in a rut while all this was going on, so it wasn't easy to get out of it. But I did.

I remember a time I was dating a new guy. It had been a while since my last serious relationship, but I was somewhat open to exploring something new. I say somewhat because things didn't start off so easily. We had different personalities but after a while it worked. It wasn't until I started dating him that I realized I changed. Things that happened in the past made it hard to trust anyone. Especially with my emotions.

To a certain extent, I'd cut my emotions off. I had no idea until he pointed it out to me one day. We went through a lot of different things and unfortunately it didn't end well. In the heat of the moment painful things were said and I just couldn't let that go. It wasn't right for someone to be putting me down and belittling me, all for finally expressing my emotions.

Now this is not to attack his character by any means. I'm just saying the situation escalated and it didn't have to. Before then I was told how I didn't care about certain things or didn't show that I cared. When I finally got the courage to express how he was making me feel, I was wrong.

Maybe things came out the wrong way, but it didn't start like that. I tried to express myself and my feelings were either unheard or not important. Things came out his mouth I'd never imagined he would say to me. I know words are not actions, but they hurt coming from someone you cared about. Especially when the words are said deliberately to hurt you.

It was a lot for me to process. I couldn't figure out why it got so hostile at the end. I thought if anything we'd had a mutual respect for each other, but I was wrong. I guess things had to go down the way it did, for me to be okay with letting it go. There were many other issues in the relationship before the incident but of course I wanted to work past them. In my mind I thought things would all work out, but we were always on two different pages.

Sometimes you have to be hurt in order to make a change. It's unfortunate but in life we take the good with the bad. It's all a part of the feeling process. Please don't tolerate anyone making you feel like you're not worthy. Trust that if things are not working out, there is a reason for it. Sometimes it's just not the right time, or you could just not be right for each other, but there are always signs. Pay attention to them. Don't discredit them because you want things to work. Once you feel that person is not for you, believe that.

You know yourself better than anyone else. So why wouldn't you trust your own gut telling you to walk away? Why would you doubt that you know what's best for you? You're the only one who can feel when something ain't right in your soul. Don't deny that.

I started to push all the negative thoughts out of my head. I went back to living every day with positive thoughts and working on being a better person. I knew there was progress still to be made internally so I started there. No, things were not the same as they were in the last phase but that didn't mean things couldn't be better. The more I began working on me, the more determined I was to make something of myself.

I self-published my first book *Remember Me* in 2016. I started my own publishing company **Built To Last Publishing LLC** and was so anxious to get to work. I already had the whole 4-part series done before I even published the first one. All I had to do was edit them and get them ready for the world to see.

It opened me back up and brought me so much joy. Becoming a published author was always a dream of mine and I felt so amazing to be doing it for myself. I knew I had so many stories to tell and could not wait to share them with the world. Going through the process of making sure every single detail is intact was definitely intense. But I loved it. Every minute of it. Still do to this day. This was something I'd never done before but my cousin gave me helpful pointers on how to self-publish. I was so excited to learn about putting something of my own out there. I felt like I was on top of the world.

Creating the LLC was like bringing new life into my world. It was such a new territory for me, and I loved learning new things about owning a business. It wasn't hard at all to get started. I was glad to be able to develop a platform to bring my stories to life. All I wanted to do was work on new ideas for the company and it felt great to be setting goals again.

For me, I needed goals to keep working towards. Whether it was self-improvement or career advancement I had to have something to keep me going. When I felt like I had nothing going on in my life I was lost. Once I started to make things happen again it gave me that push and desire to do more with my life.

So, don't be discouraged if this is where you are right now. It's necessary for you to be able to find yourself again. Make sure that you allow yourself the time to heal. It's easy to put aside taking care of ourselves mentally when we are worried about paying bills, but it's required to keep the wheels goin'. Your mind will let you know when it's time to stop and take a break. Trust your own energy. We are constantly evolving and striving to be a better person every day. As long as you continue to make sure you are happy with what you're doing in life, you'll keep shining.

If we are not moving, we are staying still and that is exactly how I felt the majority of this phase. Until I realized I didn't want to be still. I needed to keep moving. I wasn't happy staying still and my mind was letting me know that. I figured out how to shake things up and what direction I wanted to go in.

Trust yourself and trust the process. This is only a season of your life and everything will all make sense in due time. Get to know yourself at this age and don't forget what you've learned in your past years. Focus on what feels right in your soul and it will always lead you where you need to be.

Now tell me, after taking some time to reflect, what order would you prioritize the keywords from the last phase?

SOUL-SEARCHING   **GRIND**
RESPONSIBILITY

1. _______________
2. _______________
3. _______________

Why?

chapter 4: finding yourself

-Once you realize **your** potential, you're **un**stoppable-

3 Keywords in This Phase
1. acceptance
2. humility
3. power

February 14th, 2020 I woke up 30 years old in Vegas!!! Best day of my life! At first, I was nervous about turning 30 because I felt like I should've been in a different place than I was. But once the week of my birthday came, I started feeling so much clarity. Things that were foggy before were crystal clear. I'd stopped accepting people's bare minimums and reached a place of peace with taking people for who they are.

I learned years ago you can't change people, but you can change the way you deal with them. I took it upon myself to make sure I was not putting energy into anything or anyone that was not helping me succeed or putting energy into me. And I felt so great about it. 30 was like a wake-up call for me, and I didn't even know I was snoozin'. My eyes were open to seeing what was right for me. There was just no way I could accept any negativity in my life anymore.

It was the complete opposite of what I expected. Here I was thinking I was getting old, not realizing the best time of my life was just getting started. I had so much appreciation for the people who were around me because they wanted to be, not because they needed something from me. It filled me with peace to know things were shifting in my favor. I knew I had to make room for them to do so.

Things started to make perfect sense to me. I was in the space I was in because I put myself there. I was the only one who could get me out of that space I didn't want to be in anymore. I felt confident that my progress had put me in a position where I was able to accept what was for me. I knew who I was as a woman and what I should be doing with my life. I'd been through a lot of different things that brought me to that point.

There's the saying "Everybody can't go." And I never felt anything more true at the time. It was best for me to remove myself from people's lives that I no longer felt deserved to be in mine. I was the one responsible for my own feelings and I couldn't let anyone stay around me if they didn't understand that.

I've always had issues letting people go because I'm the one who keeps fighting. If I'm in your corner, I'm there for life. Up until this point it was never really a problem pouring into people that didn't pour into me. But when I realized it was holding me back, I figured out how to release.

For me, letting people go does not always mean to cut you off. It just meant the nature of certain relationships had shifted. And that was new for me, but also mandatory for me.

I took back my power over all of my thoughts and all my time. I had to make sure to put myself first. I wasn't being selfish, but maybe I needed to be. I needed to love me more in order to make these changes in my life. I never entered into a new year that made me feel so elated. I didn't know what to do with all the excitement.

It wasn't just people I had to let go of. I put away the idea of having to make sure everyone around me was situated. It had become part of a routine for me to show up for everyone else, but everyone else didn't always show up for me. I never wanted anyone to be able to say I didn't try everything possible for anyone who needed me. But once I got to the point of doing everything possible for others and I still wasn't complete, I had to walk away from that too.

Honestly it wasn't as hard as I thought it would be. It was like automatically I knew. The shit that I was accepting at 20, I couldn't be taking that at 30. The negativity and drama that seemed to find its way into my life, it was just not welcome anymore. I had no space for it. I had no desire for anything that was not contributing to my well-being anymore.

I never looked at letting things or people go as sacrifices. I looked at that task as essential. Essentially needed for my spiritual growth. For me to be able to make my life what I wanted it to be, I had to be **first**. There was no way around it. And I didn't want to make a way around it. I didn't want to make any adjustments at this age to include anything I was doing in the past that was not helping me advance.

This milestone age was all about forward movement. I couldn't move forward if I was still spending my precious time on things that would not help me excel in life. Every little thing started to develop purpose in my life and if I couldn't say what the purpose was for something, I was letting it go. I was breaking free from anything that ever held me back before and facing any fears head on.

The confidence that came along with 30 was insane! Anything I wanted I was making it happen and I knew I had what it took to get it done. My goals started to look different, but they were so exciting to think of. It fueled me to sit down and focus on where I wanted to be in the next few years. All I could think about was how to improve my life. How to put myself in a position where I would truly shine.

I felt like a grown woman. Extremely proud of the woman I'd become and so ready to keep improving. There was so much living in me left and I knew I needed to start living my life to the fullest. No reason for me to fear anything. I knew I was strong enough to handle any obstacle that came my way.

My mind, body and spirit were all telling me this is **your time**. I felt it in my bones that this next season, was for me. For me to keep up with the self-care. For me to keep publishing the rest of my books. For me to keep going through life open to new experiences and not close minded to some things I may have been before. Everything about this birthday felt different. Yes, it was my first time turning 30 but I'd never been *here* before. I say **here** in a sense of the headspace mentally. It was no teeter-tottering back and forth. No uncertainty with any decision that was made. I was so sure of every tiny detail of my life all in an instant. It was so fascinating to me because I'd never felt anything like it before.

Now I don't know you'll feel when you get to 30, or how you felt, but I can only pray you get to experience this. Even if it's just a small sample of it. This feeling is something everyone deserves. This discovery is something we all need at least once in a lifetime. This wake-up call is the one you do not want to miss. It is for you. It is for your soul. It is for your sanity.

Focus on changing for the better. You are not the person you used to be! Don't let people who have shown you who they are, convince you they are someone else. Believe what you see. You know what's best for you and you know when you something isn't right for you. We may not always want to believe something isn't for us, but time will tell.

Spend your time being devoted to yourself. To learning new things about yourself daily. To getting to know who you are at 30. We are all made up of different qualities. We all go through different phases in our life and there is no rule that says we have to stay the same. The standards I had at 20 are nothing compared to what I require now. The things I desired as a teenager are not even a thought now. But that's only because I've matured.

I'm able to see things for what they are. There is no sugar-coating anything anymore. I couldn't continue to spare feelings of people who don't even take mine into consideration. There's something so freeing that comes from shedding all that dead weight.

If you get nothing else from this phase, make sure you get this. **Peace of mind**. Acceptance and gratitude. Just because everyone can't come on your journey doesn't mean erase them from your history. The people from your past have helped shape you into the remarkable person you are today. So, you have to appreciate those for the role they played in your life.

It's all about **you** and don't let nobody tell you otherwise. Do what makes **your** heart sing. Write that book! Start that business! Take that class! Join that team! Take that trip! Get that career! Whatever your heart desires shall be yours!

Now tell me, after taking some time to reflect, what order would you prioritize the keywords from the last phase?

ACCEPTANCE   HUMILITY   POWER

1. ___________
2. ___________
3. ___________

Why?

chapter 5: serenity

-Keep calm, and stay **true** to yourself-

3 Keywords in This Phase
1. self-care
2. strength
3. appreciation

    I woke up one morning feeling like I needed to **do more**. More living, more thinking, more working. My life needed to be filled with something more than what I was doing. I needed to be doing more to help this world. I just felt like I wasn't doing as much as I could to contribute.

    2020 has definitely played a huge part in this feeling. Pandemic, riots, job loss, deaths and these are just a few words to describe what has come about. If this year has taught me anything it is to live everyday like it's your last. It's taught me to appreciate the small things we took for granted. Covid-19 came and shook us all up. I just wanted to have a moment of silence for all the lives this deadly virus has taken. And for all of my Angels Heaven has gained in the last few years. (The next page will be left blank to accommodate this remembrance.)

This year we've experienced something many have never seen in their lifetime. I know I never seen anything like it. The fear of the unknown when it came to this virus has been overwhelming to say the least. The uncertainty of the outcome is weighing heavily on so many right now. But through this storm, in the midst of all the chaos, I managed to find peace.

Peace of mind has been the most valued feeling through this crazy year we've had. You never really noticed how much you needed it before, until now. You never really saw how precious human interaction, especially between family, was until we couldn't even hug each other. You never realized how good we had it when we didn't have to wear a mask just to go to the grocery store. But now we know. And because we know this can all be taken away, we have to value it.

We need to appreciate every single moment for what it's worth. The good times of course but even the bad times. Those bad times taught you what not to do. They taught you how to think about a situation, before reacting impulsively. They taught you how to accept people as they are.

The good times taught you to crave more of them. With all the ups and downs of 2020, the good times were few and far between, so they must be cherished. Simple things like going to a show or family events, all put on hold. Yes, it's all for our safety and health, but that doesn't mean we like it.

We've learned that tomorrow is not promised, if we didn't know it before. So now is the time to live the life we deserve. Some things may still be on lockdown, but we can still find joy through this madness.

Use this time to cater to yourself. I've found more and more things to sooth me and bring quiet to this noisy world. Figure out what things you can do for yourself that make you smile. Keep up with yourself and continue getting dressed even if you working from home now. Practice different styles on your hair. Get involved with your kids virtual learning. Find activities to do around the house in your spare time.

Keep filling your days with positive thoughts and affirmations. Tell yourself you can do anything you put your mind to. This is the time you needed to finish that project or start a new one. The more we focus on what feeds our soul, the more we will keep on improving.

I've found I like to pamper myself. So what if the shops and salons are closed you'd be surprised what you can do on your own until you're forced to try. When you look good, you feel good and I truly understand that connection. **You** are the **total package** inside and out. Why not represent how you feel about yourself through self-care? Carve out time each day, just to reflect. Think about what happened throughout the day that you feel good about. Think about what happened throughout the day, you may not feel too good about. Was it anything you could have done differently? What do you think caused you to react that way? How will you make sure it goes better the next time?

I had to take a step back and ask myself all of these questions, and many more. I couldn't process exactly what was going on in my head, until I fully understood what I'd been through. This forced time at home, gave me a better view. I had the potential to bring so much more light into this dark world. I started to see myself making my dreams a reality and I loved the thought of it. So many things I said I wanted to do, and I've done them. I made it happen.

I'm beyond proud of the woman I am today. I didn't let anyone's negativity stop me from trying my best. So what they said you weren't good enough. They don't know you. So what they didn't like the color of your skin. They're intimidated by you. So what that relationship didn't work out. The next one, the **right** one, will. You never let anyone's opinions deter you, and that's what matters. People will try to bring you down, just because they are low. You don't need to stoop to their level. You're confident in yourself and don't need anyone else's approval to be yourself. To love yourself. To put yourself first.

Things fall into place when you let them. Do the work, put in the time and your reward will be miraculous. This is your show. Take control of your future and I know you'll soar to the top. The key to my serenity was all in my hands. My peace, my progress, my sanity. My mistakes, my lessons, my decisions. **It's all me**. So if I have all this power then why I am not making more happen? There's no excuse. Don't worry about if taking that leap of faith won't work out, tell yourself it will. That way making sure it does work out, is your goal.

When you want something bad enough, nothing can stand in your way. So please, **WANT** it. Want that job! Want that car, want that house! Everything you desire can be yours as long as you make it happen. Put that determination in from start to finish. Don't try to take a shortcut to speed up the process. The best part of something new is learning all about it and working your way through it. Everything in due time.

Trust in **yourself** to make your life better every day. We can't let anyone have the power to make us feel any kind of way. Happy, sad or indifferent. It is not anyone else's task to control your feelings. You are the master of your own fate and you can't afford to let yourself down.

Count on **YOU**! At the end of the day, you don't want anyone walking away with your joy. If you give them the power to be the main source of your happiness, how will you be happy when they're not around? You have to find things you can do on your own, that you love. Not to say don't welcome joy from anyone else, but don't let them dictate your peace. It's **your** life! No one can live it for you and no one will live it better than you! As long as you keep that thought in your mind, the sky is the limit!

Now tell me, after taking some time to reflect, what order would you prioritize the keywords from the last phase?

SELF-CARE   STRENGTH   APPRECIATION

1. _______________
2. _______________
3. _______________

Why?

chapter 6: hoo-rah

-I can't stress this enough-

So, you've made it this far! Congratulations! You went through so much, but you're **still** here standing. Everything you've been through was **essential** to your story. Whether you understood it or not, it was part of your path. Of course, there were some detours along the way. You had to figure out how to **love yourself.** How to feel whole, even when you're unattached. How to feel confident in walking away from a person that wasn't for you. How to demand what you deserve.

You had to figure out how to set the tone in your relationships. You attract what you exude, so put those **positive vibes** out there and see what comes back to you. You had to learn how to tell the difference between someone who needs your help and someone who's hindering you.

You figured out your worth and now know to **add tax**. You understand what you have to offer as a partner and know there is only **one you**. You are confident you made the right decision. You'll **choose you** every single time!

Our lives are full of different relationships. Before we can fully commit to any type, **you** need to be complete. You need to be secure within your own world, before you can allow anyone to be a part of it. If you're not in a state of awareness in your life where you know what you want in a spouse, how can you know what to ask for? How can you know what you will or won't take, if you don't even understand what's being offered?

Pay attention to actions. I've learned over the years people can tell you anything. And when it comes to a romantic relationship that happens more often. Watch what they **do**. People can only pretend for so long so if they're putting on a show, time will tell. If they're promising you something they can't deliver, time will tell.

Make sure you're clear on what **you want** out of life, so you can see if this person is on the same path. Do you want the same things in life? Do they want **you** in their life? A lot of people stick around because of the history. It may sometimes feel better than having to start all over with somebody new. Or it could just be easier. But why are you okay with something because it's easier? Why should you have to just take what you can get, because you love them?

Please **don't** settle! You deserve someone who wants you for you and not for what you can do for them. You deserve someone who wants the same things as you. You don't wanna be feeling like you're in this deep ass relationship and they're not even showing you that you're important. They're not making any effort to make sure you feel appreciated, so why are you going out your way to prove something to them?

I've learned people only do what **you allow**. When feelings are involved, we tend to allow more than we should. We tend to think if we give more, they'll want more. It doesn't always work like that. But if you keep giving more and more and getting less in return, something ain't right. All that says to them is that you're allowing them to give you 30% effort, while you're bending over backwards to give them 100%. Stop allowing people to take advantage of your kindness. You know they don't deserve you.

How is that fair to you? Why accept less than what you're putting out there? If you're with someone capable of returning the effort, it shouldn't be a problem to **see** that. You'd have no reason to question if you're on the same page.

Why are you okay with mediocre love when you know you deserve to be on cloud 9? You do everything and more for them, but you keep getting the short end of the stick. Time and time again you find yourself questioning if this is right for you. It **ain't!**

You know you deserve better and instead of letting better find you, you hold on to what you got hoping they'll do better. But you **know** them! And you've already shown them you're okay with minimal effort so why would they need to improve? Regardless of what you **say** when they show you how they really feel about you, you still find a way to justify the disrespect.

They're watching your actions and don't give a damn about what you're saying. Because last time you said it was over, but it's still going on. Last time you said you weren't dealing with them with no more, and here you are back dealing with them. You were extremely vocal about how they couldn't make you a priority, but now you're okay being an afterthought.

If things ain't workin' out, there's a reason things ain't workin' out. Sometimes things have to fall apart, for better things to fall in place. We do not have to stay with someone simply because of the time invested. If you are not on the same page it is not going to work. You can't be over here planning things for **y'all** to do, while all they focused on is what **they** want to do.

Loving somebody harder will not make them get it together. It will not force someone to do right by you, if that's not what they want to do. Stop takin' care of people who ain't takin' care of you. Feelings are to be **felt**. If you and the person you're with are feeling the same about each other, you're going to see it. You'll know it. You will feel it. When one of you start to feel differently, you'll see that too. Sometimes we outgrow people and don't even notice it. All we can see is that we love this person so much it has to work. But what if it's not meant to work?

You have so much to bring to the table. If the person you eatin' with can't see that, find **another** table. You're loving yourself at the

highest capacity. Why would it be okay to allow someone to love you at any level less than that? They have to measure up.

Please stop trying to make things more than they are. If they showed you they can't be dependable, believe it. This is what **you're** seeing. With **your own** two eyes. When did you start doubting your own vision? These are their actions. And anyone who cares about you wouldn't let you down. They'd make sure you felt the love and appreciation.

People make time for who they want and what they want. If they're not making time for you, they don't want to. Don't let anybody convince you they are busy 24/7. And if they can't make time for you, don't you make time for them.

Be okay with walking away from love when it's no longer healthy. You know when things aren't right. It may be hard to accept but trust how you feel. Take time to be alone and prepare yourself for your match. Make sure you're at your best level to let in the one you're supposed to be with.

Choose your sanity over anybody that don't appreciate you. Believe it is not worth your peace, to be with someone who don't know or care to know you're worth. It's okay to be alone from time to time. Don't hop from relationship to relationship just because you don't want to be alone. You're not doing yourself any favors skipping over the much needed "me-time" in between relationships.

I say all this to say, **celebrate you**! Make the decision to put yourself first every day. It's all about finding ways to bring joy into your life. You have to put those positive vibes in the atmosphere and tell yourself, "Today, I'm gonna be happy." Regardless of the headache you woke up with or the argument you had with so-and-so yesterday, you are going to be happy today. Tell yourself every day. Whatever obstacles come your way cannot take away your smile. Please don't let them take away your smile. You've pushed through set-backs and heartbreaks and you deserve to be full of joy every day. Because **you** didn't let any of the things that hurt you, **break you**. Because **you** didn't stop fighting for your goals, even when the road got tough. Because **you** persevered even when they said you couldn't do it. Look back at your life and tell yourself **thank you**. **You** made this happen, because **you** wanted it. So if you're looking for a way to be happy, just want it a little more. We all say we **want** to be happy, but how bad do we really want it? Are we willing to put in the work to keep the tranquility in our everyday lives? Can we continue to make sure that other people's negativity does not determine our mood? I know **you** can! You've been doing it all along!

SELF EVALUATION

Through my process of self-reflection I found myself with these few questions. If you have the time, take a minute to reflect on these phases, or any other aspect of your life and jot down your answers. Even if you do nothing with this, answer truthfully.

1. If you had the opportunity to re-do any of these phases in life for one week, which one would you choose? Why?

2. Do you feel comfortable creating your own joy?

3. Do you know what you want out of life?

4. Are you willing to do whatever it takes to get it?

5. Are you happy in this current stage of your life?

If your answer is no, why not?

If your answer is yes, how will you continue to make sure you're happy?